How Did THIS Happen HERE?

Leni Donlan

Chicago, Illinois

Designed by Kimberly R. Miracle and Betsy Wernert
Photo Research by Tracy Cummins
Map on page 14 by Mapping Specialists
Printed and bound in the United States of America, North Mankato, MN.

13 12 11
10 9 8 7 6 5 4 3 2

Library of Congress Cataloging-in-Publication Data
Donlan, Leni.
  How did this happen here? : Japanese internment camps / Leni Donlan.
      p. cm. -- (American history through primary sources)
  Includes bibliographical references and index.
  ISBN 978-1-4109-2701-9 (hbk.) -- ISBN 978-1-4109-2712-5 (pbk.)
  1. Japanese Americans--Evacuation and relocation, 1942-1945--Juvenile literature. 2. World War, 1939-1945--Japanese Americans--Juvenile literature. 3. World War, 1939-1945--Concentration camps--United States--Juvenile literature. 4. Concentration camps--United States--History--Juvenile literature. I. Title. II. Title: Japanese internment camps.
  D769.8.A6D65 2008
  940.53'1773--dc22
  022011   2007005911
  006055R

Acknowledgments
The author and publisher are grateful to the following for permission to reproduce copyright material: Bettmann/CORBIS p. 4; Courtesy of National Archives **pp. 5, 6 (left), 6 (right), 13, 16, 16–17, 18 (top), 18–19, 19 (top), 28**; Library of Congress Prints and Photographs Division **pp. 7, 8, 9, 10, 11 (top), 11 (bottom), 12, 15 (right), 15 (left), 17, 20, 21, 22 (left), 22 (right), 23, 25 (top), 25 (bottom), 29**; Army Center for Military History file photo **pp. 26, 27**.

Cover image of Tule Lake Relocation Center, Newell California, reproduced with permission of National Archives.

The publishers would like to thank William Yoshino of the Japanese American Citizens League and Nancy Harris for their assistance in the preparation of this book.

Every effort has been made to contact copyright holders of any material reproduced in this book. Any omissions will be rectified in subsequent printings if notice is given to the publishers.

Contents

Some words are printed in bold, **like this**. You can find out what they mean on page 30. You can also look in the box at the bottom of the page where they first appear.

World War II

In 1941 a lot of the world was at war. The United States was far away from the terrible fighting. It thought it was safe from danger. That changed on December 7, 1941. The time was 7:53 in the morning.

That was when a surprise attack was made on the United States. It was made by the country of Japan. Japan attacked the U.S. naval base on Hawaii. The base was in Pearl Harbor. The attack killed 2,403 Americans. The United States lost 188 planes. It also lost eight battleships. Now, Americans knew that distance did not make them safe.

This map shows the island of Oahu in Hawaii. You can see where Pearl Harbor is.

The American people were shocked. Many Americans were angry. Most were frightened and sad.

President Franklin D. Roosevelt led the country at that time. He said that the United States was at war. Americans were sent far away to fight. The United States was now a part of World War II.

Changes took place inside the United States, too. The way Americans lived and worked changed. The changes were hard on all Americans. But some Americans suffered more than others.

The USS *Shaw* was one of the U.S. ships at Pearl Harbor. This picture was taken as the ship blew up.

Executive Order 9066

Americans feared another attack from Japan. They considered Japan an enemy. Some people worried about the Japanese Americans. They did not like them living in the United States. They felt they might be dangerous. They wanted the government leaders to make the country safe.

Signs like this said that Japanese Americans had to leave their homes. They had to go to special camps during World War II.

EXECUTIVE ORDER

- - - - - - -

AUTHORIZING THE SECRETARY OF WAR TO PRESCRIBE MILITARY AREAS

WHEREAS the successful prosecution of the war requires every possible protection against espionage and against sabotage to national-defense material, national-defense premises, and national-defense utilities as defined in Section 4, Act of April 20, 1918, 40 Stat. 533, as amended by the Act of November 30, 1940, 54 Stat. 1220, and the Act of August 21, 1941, 55 Stat. 655 (U. S. C., Title 50, Sec. 104):

NOW, THEREFORE, by virtue of the authority vested in me as President of the United States, and Commander in Chief of the Army and Navy, I hereby authorize and direct the Secretary of War, and the Military Commanders whom he may from time to time designate, whenever he or any designated Commander deems such action necessary or desirable, to prescribe military areas in such places and of such extent as he or the appropriate Military Commander may determine, from which any or all persons may be excluded, and with which, the right of any person to enter, re- whatever restric-

WESTERN DEFENSE COMMAND AND FOURTH ARMY
WARTIME CIVIL CONTROL ADMINISTRATION
Presidio of San Francisco, California
April 1, 1942

INSTRUCTIONS TO ALL PERSONS OF JAPANESE ANCESTRY

Living in the Following Area:

All that portion of the City and County of San Francisco, State of California, lying generally west of the north-south line established by Junipero Serra Boulevard, Worchester Avenue, and Nineteenth Avenue, and lying generally north of the east-west line established by California Street, to the intersection of Market Street, and thence on Market Street to San Francisco Bay.

All Japanese persons, both alien and non-alien, will be evacuated from the above designated area by 12:00 o'clock noon Tuesday, April 7, 1942.

No Japanese person will be permitted to enter or leave the above described area after 8:00 a. m., Thursday, April 2, 1942, without obtaining special permission from the Provost Marshal at the Civil Control Station located at:

1701 Van Ness Avenue
San Francisco, California

The Civil Control Station is equipped to assist the Japanese population affected by this evacuation in the following ways:

Give advice and instructions on the evacuation.

Provide services with respect to the management, leasing, sale, storage or other disposition of most kinds of property, including: real estate, business and professional equipment, buildings, household goods, boats, automobiles,

Provide temporary residence elsewhere for all Japanese in family groups.

Transport persons and a limited amount of clothing and equipment to their new residence, as specified below.

6

executive order	rule made by a president that has the force of law
injustice	making people suffer as a result of something, such as a law, that is not right or fair
internment camp	large prison where people who are thought to be dangerous to the country are kept in time of war

This man was forced to leave his home.

President Roosevelt signed **Executive Order** 9066 on February 19, 1942. An executive order is a rule made by a president. It is like a law that people had to follow. The order gave the government unusual power. They said this power was needed to make the United States safe.

The order was about Japanese Americans who lived in the United States. It said they had to move. They were forced to live in **internment camps**. These were special camps. The camps kept Japanese Americans closed in. They kept them guarded. The government said that Japanese Americans might be spies for Japan. Henry L. Stimson, the U.S. secretary of war, explained: "We cannot understand or trust...[the] Japanese."

People's fears led them to deny Japanese Americans their rights. They lost their freedom. As a result, Japanese Americans suffered a great **injustice**.

Fear, Shame, and Loss

About 120,000 Japanese Americans were sent to **internment camps** (large prisons). This happened during World War II. More than two-thirds of them were U.S. **citizens**. Citizens are people who live in a country. They are supposed to be protected by the laws (rules) of their country. Half of these Japanese were children. Most of the children were born in the United States. They had lived in the United States all their lives.

Japanese Americans lost their businesses.

citizen   person who lives in a country and is protected by the laws of that country
convict   find guilty of a crime in a court of law

These children are all Americans. They were unfairly treated as enemies of their country.

Dangerous?

During World War II, a few people were **convicted** of spying for Japan. None of the people found guilty were Japanese Americans. Japanese Americans were not a danger to their country.

Before the war, Japanese-American citizens were proud to live in the United States. They were happy to live there. But during the war, they were not treated as citizens. They lost their homes and businesses. They lost their hope and their honor.

Sometimes family members were sent to separate internment camps. When that happened, they even lost their families.

Relocation

Every Japanese American had to **register** with the U.S. government. This means their names were put on a list. They were each given an **identification** number. These numbers said who each person was. This happened in the spring of 1942

Posted orders told them when and where to gather. The gathering places were called **assembly centers**. These centers were filthy. Japanese Americans were sent from the centers to **internment camps**. These were like large prisons.

These Japanese Americans are waiting to register.

assembly center	guarded places where Japanese Americans were first sent. They went there before they went to internment camps.
identification	something that says who a person is
register	to get one's name put on a special list

Leaving home was hard for Japanese Americans. They could only take what they could carry with their hands. They stuffed as much as they could into suitcases and bags.

Some families were lucky. Friends or neighbors cared for their homes and their pets. Most Japanese Americans lost almost everything they owned.

Imagine what this would have been like. What would you take if you had to leave your home like this?

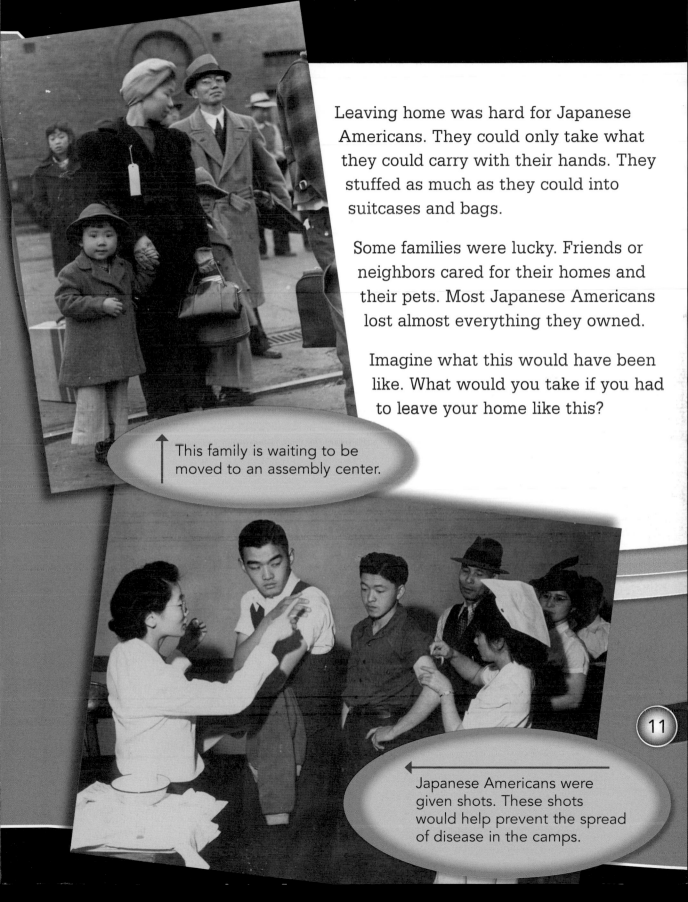

This family is waiting to be moved to an assembly center.

Japanese Americans were given shots. These shots would help prevent the spread of disease in the camps.

Assembly centers

Assembly centers were the first stop for Japanese Americans. Some people came on foot. Others came by car or truck. And some came by bus or train. Assembly centers were large public areas. They could be fairgrounds or racetracks. Japanese Americans had to stay in cowsheds and horse stalls. They lived there for many months. These homes were very dirty. Hunger, cold, and illness were common.

After staying in assembly centers, Japanese Americans were put on trains. The trains went to internment camps.

cot   small bed that can be folded up

These children are on a train with 600 others. They are being moved to an internment camp.

Mae Ninomiya, a Japanese-American woman, tells about her experience. "Let me begin my story from the assembly center.... This was the place we entered in May of 1942. We were housed in a barn where the animals had been placed.... The only furniture was the six **cots** [small beds] for our family of six. Our clothes were in two suitcases we were allowed for the entire family." Mae's family stayed in the assembly center until September 1942.

Saku Tomita was in a different assembly center. She reported: "Today we did not have any bread for lunch or dinner, either. I did not have enough to eat."

Destinations

Japanese Americans stayed in **assembly centers** for months. Then they were moved again. They were moved to **internment camps**. There were ten internment camps in the United States. These camps kept Japanese Americans in certain places. They were like prisons.

Japanese Americans had to go to the camps. They had no choice. They could not leave the camps. Guards watched them all the time.

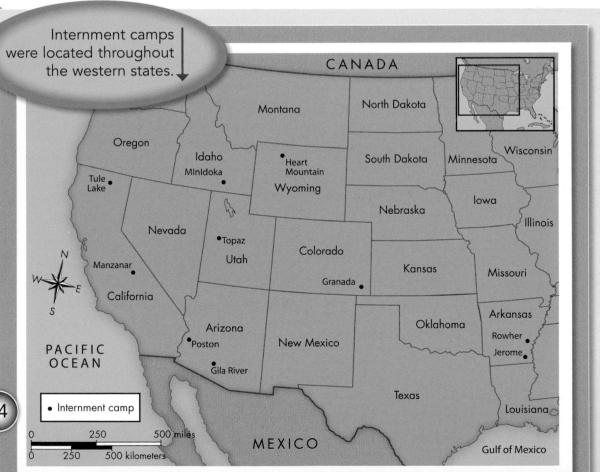

Internment camps were located throughout the western states.

barrack   building or group of buildings used to house soldiers
mess hall   large dining room where everyone eats. Mess halls are usually for soldiers.
remote   apart from other places

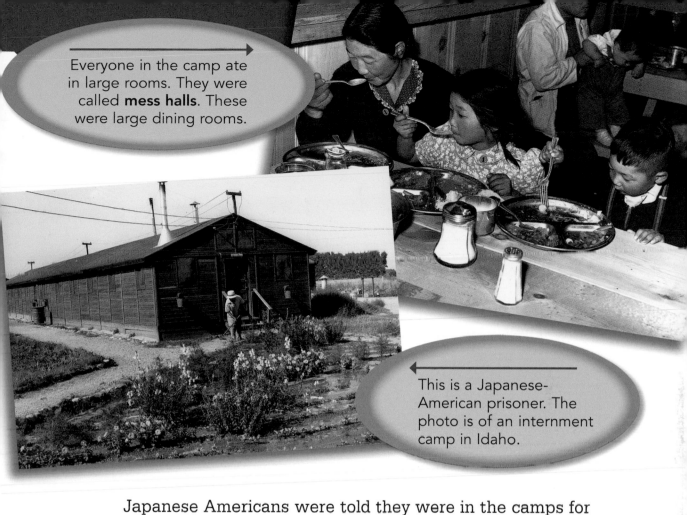

Everyone in the camp ate in large rooms. They were called **mess halls**. These were large dining rooms.

This is a Japanese-American prisoner. The photo is of an internment camp in Idaho.

Japanese Americans were told they were in the camps for "their own protection." But, as one Japanese American said: "If we were put there for our protection, why were the guns at the guard towers pointed inward, instead of outward?"

The camps were built very quickly. They were not built well. They were in **remote** areas. They were located many miles away from other cities. Many families shared each **barrack**. A barrack is usually a building used by soldiers. There was little privacy in internment camps. There was also little comfort.

Japanese Americans tried to make the best of things. They continued to hope for a better future.

15

The Camps

Living in the camps was hard for Japanese Americans. Here is what some of them were like. See the map on page 14 to see where they were.

Tule Lake held nearly 19,000 **internees**. An internee is a person kept in one place.

Manzanar Camp was on the edge of a large desert. The summers were burning hot. The winters were freezing. The wind always blew. Manzanar held around 10,000 internees.

Poston Camp was also known as Colorado River Camp.

Topaz Camp was in the middle of an area where nothing grew. Topaz opened in September 1942. It closed in October 1945.

Poston Camp was open from May 1942 to November 1945. It held nearly 18,000 internees.

Minidoka Camp was burning hot in the summer. It was freezing cold in the winter. One person who lived there said: "When we first arrived here we almost cried, and thought that this is the land God had forgotten." It held about 13,000 internees.

internee   person who is kept in one place, especially in time of war

Tule Lake Camp was even more like a prison than the other **internment camps**.

A large mountain range could be seen from Manzanar Camp.

17

Granada Camp was dry and dusty.

Heart Mountain Camp was in an area without trees and with little water.

18

Rohwer Camp was built on swampland.

More camps

Gila River Camp may have been the nicest **internment camp**. Its special roofs protected the buildings. The roofs kept out the desert heat. This camp held more than 13,000 internees.

Heart Mountain Camp had some of the worst weather. More than 10,000 **internees** lived there.

Granada (or Amache) Camp was the smallest camp. Granada had terrible snowstorms in the winter. But it also had cool mountain breezes in the summer. Granada housed about 7,500 internees.

Jerome Camp was in the middle of **swampland**. It had muddy land with standing water. It was very **humid**, meaning it had damp, warm air. It got almost 60 inches (152 centimeters) of rain a year. Mud and snakes were big problems there. So were mosquitoes and diseases. Many people got sick. It housed nearly 8,500 internees.

Rohwer Camp's internees also suffered from heat. They suffered from humidity and rain. Rohwer also housed about 8,500 internees.

Life in the Camps

What was life like for Japanese Americans behind the **internment camp** fences?

Internees did all kinds of work in the camps. Internment camps ran farms. The food grown was often traded between camps. Internees did other jobs, too. Sometimes they worked for pay. But pay was low.

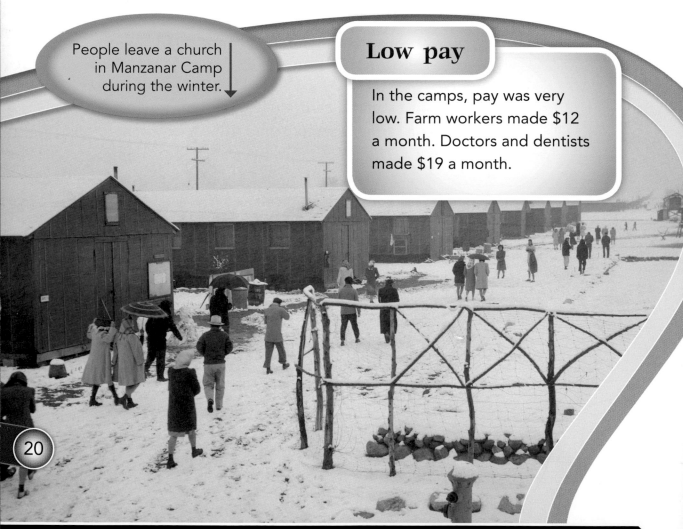

People leave a church in Manzanar Camp during the winter.

Low pay

In the camps, pay was very low. Farm workers made $12 a month. Doctors and dentists made $19 a month.

20

This artist was forced to live in Manzanar camp.

Internees did all the jobs needed to run the camp. They cooked and cleaned. They sewed and built furniture.

They worked as **journalists**. They wrote for newspapers and magazines. They worked as musicians and artists. Professional artists offered classes in many camps. Through art and writing, internees were able to share their feelings. They could show how they felt about being forced to live in the camps.

Making the best of it

Life could be very boring in the camps. So **internees** formed sports teams and clubs. They made gardens and grew food. They had bakeries and small stores. They provided medical services. They created churches and Sunday schools.

Each camp had schools for children. Camp schools did not have enough books. They didn't have enough school **supplies**. They needed pencils and paper. Somehow, they made do with what they had.

It was not easy to raise a child in the camps. Parents did what they could. They tried to make life good for their children.

These men are bakers at a store in one of the camps.

22

isolation — being away from other people
searchlight — bright light that can turn to shine on a large area
supplies — things needed for teaching and learning, such as paper, maps, pencils, and pens

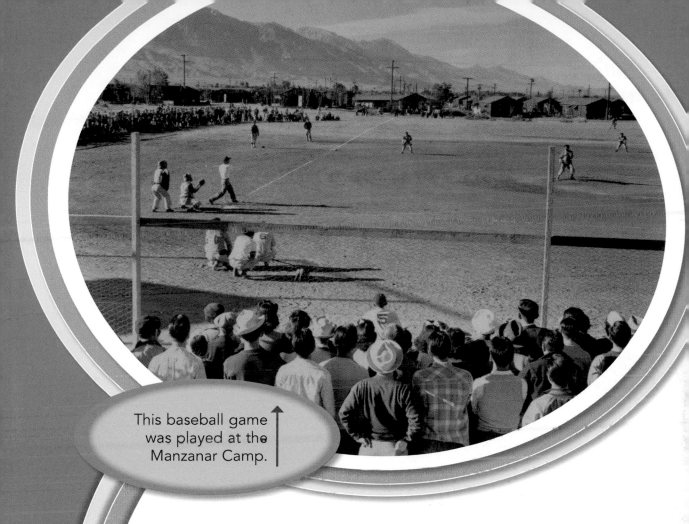

This baseball game was played at the Manzanar Camp.

Japanese-American internees made the best of their bad situation. But internees were very unhappy. They were unhappy about the bad housing. They were unhappy about the foods they had to eat. They were unhappy about the **isolation** of their camps. They were far from other people. They were unhappy about the guard towers. They were unhappy about the **searchlights**. The searchlights shined day and night on them. They were unhappy that they lost their freedom.

23

The Internees speak

Japanese-American **internees** left nice homes. They left successful lives. They had to move to places far away. They were far away from everything they knew. Guards carried guns. They watched the internees all the time. Somehow, the internees made a life for themselves.

The following are some of their memories:
"The food might all stop one day, and it gave me very uneasy and uncomfortable feelings to see the guards watching us from the **tower**. We were fenced in. I couldn't take my eyes off my children... so that they would not go outside the fence. The guards were to shoot anyone that did." —Internee

"There was [no] privacy.... One had to get used to snores, baby-crying, family troubles." —Mine Okubo, an internee

An internee's poem

Snow upon the rooftop
Snow upon the coal
Winter in Wyoming
Winter in my soul
      —Miyuki Aoyama
Aoyama wrote this poem while at Heart Mountain Camp.

tower   tall structure used to look down and watch an area

Internees elect (choose) officers to lead in their camp government.

Internees shared their skills and talents. This is a dressmaking class at Manzanar Camp. The teacher and students are internees.

Loyalty

The government did not think of the Japanese Americans as **citizens**. The government thought they were enemies. Japanese Americans were thought of as "enemy **aliens**" by the government. This means they were not protected by the laws of the United States.

This is a photo of the 442nd Regimental Combat Team. They won thousands of awards for their brave work in World War II.

alien   someone who is not a citizen

The 442nd Regimental Combat Team saved the lives of 211 U.S. soldiers.

The governement asked Japanese Americans in the camps to join the U.S. Army. Japanese Americans could not agree on what to do.

Most Japanese Americans were angry. Many were shocked when they were asked to join the army. Some said they would not join the army. They would not join unless their rights were returned. They wanted to be treated like any other citizens. Why would the U.S. government ask them to fight for the freedom of others? The government had taken away their freedom!

Some Japanese Americans did agree to serve in the army. Many of them served in the 442nd Regimental Combat Team. The combat team received many medals for bravery and honor.

Would you have fought for a country that treated you so unfairly?

After the War

World War II ended in 1945. Japanese Americans could leave the camps. Many Japanese Americans had no home to go back to. They had no job to go back to. Many Japanese Americans started new lives in new places.

In 1988 the U.S. government said that Japanese-American **internment camps** were wrong. The government said it was sorry for the way it had treated Japanese Americans.

No one wanted to leave their homes to live in the internment camps. The U.S. government forced them to.

concept	idea
dignity	getting respect from others
faith	believing in something

Huge losses

Japanese Americans lost homes and businesses worth billions of dollars during World War II.

Earl Warren was in California's government during the war. He thought the internment camps were a good idea. Later, Warren changed his mind. He said: "It was not in keeping with our American **concept** [idea] of freedom and the rights of **citizens**." He meant that the United States did not treat the Japanese Americans fairly.

Frank Kitamoto and his family were in a camp. He said this about Japanese Americans during the war: "They lost their property. They lost their **dignity** and **faith** in America and what it stood for." He meant that the United States did not treat Japanese Americans with any repsect. They no longer believed in what the United States stood for.

Could something like this happen in the United States again?

Japanese Americans were glad to leave places like Manzanar Camp.

Glossary

alien someone who is not a citizen of the country they live in

assembly center place where Japanese Americans were sent for a time. They went there before they went to internment camps.

barrack building or group of buildings used to house soldiers

citizen person who lives in a country and is protected by the laws of that country

concept idea

condition way something is, such as the weather or the quality of housing

convict find guilty of a crime in a court of law

cot small bed that can be folded up

dignity getting respect from others

executive order rule made by a president that has the force of law

faith believing in something

humid having damp, warm air

identification something that says who a person is

injustice making people suffer as a result of something, such as a law, that is not right or fair

internee person who is kept in one place, especially in time of war

internment camp place where people who are considered dangerous to the country are kept in time of war

isolation being away from other people

journalist writer for newspapers and magazines

mess hall large dining room where everyone eats. Mess halls are usually for soldiers.

register get one's name put on a special list

remote apart from other places

searchlight bright light that can turn to shine on a large area

supplies things needed for teaching and learning, such as paper, maps, pencils, and pens

swampland land that is muddy and has standing water

tower tall structure used to look down and watch an area

Want to Know More?

Books to read

- Bunting, Eve. *So Far from the Sea*. New York: Clarion, 1998.
- Mochizuki, Ken. *Baseball Saved Us*. New York: Lee & Low, 1993.
- Tunnell, Michael O., and George W. Chilcoat. *The Children of Topaz: The Story of a Japanese-American Internment Camp*. New York: Holiday House, 1996.

Websites

- http://memory.loc.gov/learn/lessons/99/fear/interview.html
  Marielle Tsukamoto tells about her time in the internment camp in Jerome, Arkansas.
- http://www.americaslibrary.gov/cgi-bin/page.cgi/jb/wwii/pearlhar_1
  Learn about America's reaction to the bombing of Pearl Harbor.

Places to visit

- **Manzanar Camp**
  (760) 878-2194 ext. 2710
  This camp is now run by the National Park service. You can see what it was like. It's located in Independence, CA.

- **Pearl Harbor**
  (808) 487-3327
  Visit the Pearl Harbor Memorial and Museum.

Read **When Will I Get In?: Segregation and Civil Rights** to find out about the struggle against segregation and Jim Crow laws.

Read **Varian Fry: Hero of the Holocaust** to find out about this brave American who risked his life to rescue refugees in France.

Index